ravin driftwood

FALL REMINDS US THAT CHANGE IS BEAUTIFUL

this is fall

Illustration Engineer: Ravin Driftwood
Book Cover Design: SPIRIT FLOW DESIGN, LLC
www.etsy.com/shop/spiritflowdesign
Publisher: MOUNTAIN GOAT PUBLICATIONS
www.amazon.com/author/mountaingoat

MOUNTAIN GOAT
PUBLICATIONS